A VICTOR'S Heart

A VICTOR'S Heart

Unlocking the Chambers of Love, Forgiveness, and Trust to Obtain Abundant Life

Cassandra L. Williams

A VICTOR'S HEART
UNLOCKING THE CHAMBERS OF LOVE, FORGIVENESS, AND TRUST TO OBTAIN ABUNDANT LIFE

iUniverse books may be ordered through booksellers or by contacting:

iUniverse
1663 Liberty Drive
Bloomington, IN 47403
www.iuniverse.com
1-800-Authors (1-800-288-4677)

ISBN: 978-1-4917-5335-4 (sc)
ISBN: 978-1-4917-5334-7 (e)

Library of Congress Control Number: 2014921821

Printed in the United States of America.

iUniverse rev. date: 12/31/2014

ACKNOWLEDGMENTS

"Now unto Him that is able to do exceedingly and abundantly above all we could ever ask or think according to the Spirit that works in us" (Ephesians 3:20). I would like to thank God for entrusting me with the honor of writing this devotional to help others.

To my parents, John and Elvira Rogers and Willie Malcolm, thank you for all of your love, support, and patience with me in life and this process. You did your best, and it was good enough. I can never repay you for all that you have done for me, but I hope my life brings you much joy.

To my grandmother Pearlie Mae Young, you are gone but never forgotten. You will never hold this in your hands in the natural, but you were my angel throughout this process. When I wanted to quit, I could hear you say, "Keep going. You can do it." You stood by me every step of the way and sent me a special friend who embodies your spirit. Granny, this is your legacy.

To Nicole Alexander and Mary Nuckles, thank you for allowing me to travel on this journey with you. Your love and passion ignited a dream I thought had passed me by. I wouldn't have done this without you. We helped each other complete the process instead of competing with one another. I am eternally grateful and wish you much success with your own projects.

To Darcel Summleor, the first person to prophecy concerning me writing a book. Your words did not fall on deaf ears. It has taken years to get here, but I made it. It was an honor to pray with you all those years.

To my spiritual leaders, Pastors Myles and DeLana Rutherford, Jerome and LaTunya Dial, and my Worship with Wonders family, your love helped me heal and have the strength to finish. Your messages taught us to trust God and to dream big. Your example is one that pushes us to want more and to go farther than the status quo. It may not always seem like we are listening, but let this be a sign that we hear and believe the God in you.

> The [uncompromisingly] righteous shall flourish like the palm tree [be long-lived, stately, upright, useful, and fruitful]; they shall grow like a cedar in Lebanon [majestic,

stable, durable, and incorruptible]. Planted in the House of the Lord, they shall flourish in the courts of our God.

[Growing in grace] they shall still bring forth fruit in old age; they shall be full of sap [of spiritual vitality] and [rich in the] verdure [of trust, love, and contentment].

[They are living memorials] to show that the Lord is upright *and* faithful to His promises; He is my rock, and there is no unrighteousness in Him. (Psalm 92:12–15 Amplified Bible)

CONTENTS

INTRODUCTION

As I drove to work on October 14, 2009, I did not listen to the radio or get on my cell phone as I often did. I had been praying to God about situations in my life. My main request was not for money or material things. I wanted more of Him. I wanted to know more about this person who loved me enough to send His Son to die for me. I wanted to be the person that He had prophesied I could be. I wanted to live the life of abundance that He talked about in John 10:10.

As I continued to drive, I heard the words "chambers of love." I immediately prayed and asked God what it all meant. He answered me with a mental picture. I was standing in front of this object that looked like the human heart (the real thing—not the cute pictures we draw) with a key in my hand. I looked around for the opening and could not find it.

A voice said, "Lie down on the floor."

I found a door. I had to crawl in from the floor. As I entered the object, there were four different chambers. There was just enough room for me to get in. It was tight, and the only way out was to go into the next chamber. You could not even turn around. I could only stand up and pull myself out in the last chamber.

♥ INTERPRETATION

To understand the heart of God and reach that abundant life God has promised, we cannot do it standing up. I am not talking about your physical position. I am talking about your spiritual posture. Yes, the veil has been ripped, and we can come boldly to the throne of God to make our requests known unto Him.

In this season, however, we must humble ourselves to enter into the heart of God. This will appear to be a very lonely time for you because you will have to leave your spouse, children, family, friends, work, and anyone or anything that could be a distraction. There is only enough room for one on this journey. The process is so designed that you cannot go back. You can only go forward to the next chamber. When you emerge, you will understand the heart of God and have the mind of Christ. Just as Christ's only desire was to do the will of the Father, so shall your desire be.

Let's take a look at the four chambers to get a brief description of each one. The first chamber is love. This is the first thing we learn about God, and it sustains us through the other chambers. The second chamber is forgiveness. This is where we learn to let go of past hurts and disappointments and forgive God, others, and ourselves. The third chamber is trust. This is where we learn to submit our will to God and trust Him in every area to lead and guide us. We learn to trust His voice and do things differently, which leads to the fourth chamber: abundant life. This is where we learn to live life in abundance (to the fullest, until it overflows).

This book will provoke you to think and stretch your mind and theology about the heart of God. I cannot tell you that this process will be easy. I cannot tell you that this process will be comfortable. I cannot tell you how long the process will take. I can tell you that you will cry. You will get angry, and you will want to quit.

In these moments, remember the words of Dan Millman in *Peaceful Warrior*. "The journey is what brings us happiness not the destination." When I began to write this book, I naively thought I had lived through this phase of my life. I trusted God to give me the words to say, but now I realize I had only touched the surface. This is a journey that we will be taking together.

An expert or authority is not always the person with the plaques and degrees on his or her walls. I have taken several classes at a local seminary during my eleven years in ministry. I have studied and taught countless Bible studies, led women's ministry groups, and assisted several pastors as their assistant, but none of that prepared me to write this book. The power and anointing behind the words comes from God because I have had to live every word. This was not a book that I sat down and wrote in a month or two. This book has taken twists and turns over the years and opened my spiritual eyes and my natural eyes. I am just like you. I have had to overcome situations that seemed insurmountable. I have had to unlock the hidden chambers to be able to live the life God ordained for me.

In this book, I share my stories about how I felt and dealt with each of the chambers. There are spaces for you to write your stories. How did you feel when certain things did or did not happen? How did you cope? Are you over it—or are you still dealing with certain situations? I have included spaces for your truth—whatever that truth may be. This will allow you to gauge where you are personally on this journey.

As you write, remember the words of William Shakespeare: "to thy own self be true." This is not the time to dance around the issues. It is time to dig up the roots that have held you hostage in a place God never created for you to grow in. Submission is not a destination that we reach. It is a state that we live in every day as believers.

No matter what awaits you at the end of this journey, just relax and enjoy it. Know that when you come out into abundant life, it will all be worth it.

Chamber 1
LOVE

*W*e search for it, and we dream about it. Some people have even thought about killing for it. I am talking about *love*—that feeling of complete comfort, connection, and security in knowing that if you fall, there is someone there to catch you. If you cry, someone is there to wipe away the tears. When you are all alone and all hell is breaking loose in your life and you feel like you cannot hold on anymore, a voice says, "I got you. Just let go and rest."

You know that feeling you have during the holidays when you are sitting around with the children playing, people laughing, and mass quantities of all your favorite foods. In those priceless moments, you smile because you realize that you have everything you need. That feeling you miss when the matriarch or a special loved one is no longer around. That kind of love is not based on reciprocity. I am talking about God's unconditional love. We long for this love to come from within. We have sought this love from a man—or maybe a woman—and were left disappointed. We often cannot handle this kind of love because it is pure and untainted. This love transforms us from the inside out.

As much as you have longed for Him, He longed for you enough to send His only Son to die for you. He knew your end before your beginning. Nothing in your life has caught Him by surprise, and He wants you to know that you are *His love*. Let's see if it aligns with our reality of love:

> Love is patient (another translation says long suffering) and kind. Love is not jealous or boastful or proud or rude. It does not demand its own way. It is not irritable, and it keeps no record of being wronged. It does not rejoice about injustice but rejoices whenever the truth wins out. Love never gives up, never loses faith, is always hopeful, and endures through every circumstance. (1 Corinthians 13:4–7 New Living Translation)

Even as I read these lines today, this is not my reality. I fall short *daily*—sometimes two or three times—but

God continues to extend His grace and mercy to me. He is the perfect example of how we are supposed to love. What do I mean? Think about your life. Only you know the path you have had to walk. Think of all the times you did not want to do what God wanted you to do. Maybe you had the courage to tell Him that you did not want to do this or that, but He continued to pursue you with an everlasting love that drew you to Him (Jeremiah 31:3).

God was relentless in proving Himself to you. You prayed, and He answered. You cried, and He wiped away your tears. You needed to talk, and He listened. You were lonely, and He had nowhere He would rather be. You had a need, and He provided. He wooed you. No matter how bad you thought you were—or people confirmed you were—He still loved you so much that He gave His only begotten Son (John 3:16).

Let's take a moment for a praise break right there. I do not know anyone who would give his or her only son to die for another person, knowing that the person would reject him. Even when we are guilty, He continues to cover us. In my life, I have found that to be difficult. Sometimes you have to cover for people who are persecuting you or accusing you of wrongdoing.

Sometimes when people accuse you of things, you have to look at the people that are around you. Why? You can be found guilty by association. If you hang around gossipers—whether you say a word or not—people will assume you are just like them. My grandmother used to say, "Be careful of the company you keep."

> "Can two walk together except they agree"
> (Amos 3:3 KJV).

Look at the people around you. A common thread binds you to them. If it is not the Holy Spirit once that thread is broken (by life, healing, or deliverance), you will separate. Sometimes God comes in and breaks that thread because a person is traveling in your blind spot.

> blind Spot: A small area of the retina where the optic nerve enters the eye; this type of blind spot occurs normally in all eyes; a part of an area that cannot be directly observed under existing circumstances; an area where radio reception is weak or nonexistent; a subject about which one is markedly ignorant or prejudiced.
>
> (American Heritage Dictionary online)

You may be so close to a person or sympathize with him or her so much that you miss the whole picture. You may have a person in your life who helped you or who you helped through a really tough time (death in the family, divorce, etc.). Perhaps that person even led you to Christ. You remember the good things, but you cannot see how negative and judgmental he or she can be or how he or she gossips about everyone around him or her. Every time you talk to your "friend," you feel drained. When people see you with this person, they see you as negative or judgmental. You may even take on their tendencies if you are not strong enough in the Word of God. People come into your life for a reason, a season, or a lifetime. Sometimes separation comes to save your life.

"Do not let your good be spoken of as evil" (Romans 14:6 NKJ).

"One bad apple spoils the bunch" (1 Corinthians 5:6 NKJ).

Noah, a man of the soil, proceeded to plant a vineyard. When he drank some of its wine, he became drunk and lay uncovered inside his tent. Ham, the father of Canaan, saw his father naked and told his two brothers outside. But Shem and Japheth took a garment and laid it across their shoulders; then they walked in backward and covered their father's naked body. Their faces were turned the other way so that they would not see their father naked. (Genesis 9:20–23 NIV)

Ham represents many people in our lives and the Body of Christ that see the faults of others and run and tell others to bring shame and disgrace. They gossip instead of praying. They judge instead of covering. They are religious instead of valuing relationship. Shem and Japheth represent how we should respond to information when it is brought to us. They never turned to look upon their father. They believed what was said, placed the garment (prayer in the spiritual sense) over their shoulders, backed in, and covered their father.

It is amazing how we can have more loyalty in the world than we do in the church. I did not have many close friends growing up. My inner circle was—and still is—very small. However, if you could make it into that circle and be considered a friend, you had my loyalty until the end or until you betrayed me. We would fight together, and right or wrong would be determined in private. We'll talk more about this when we deal with the trust factor.

The three brothers loved their father and did not want to see his sin. Notice how they never said it wasn't there—they just did not dwell upon it. This is tight even for me, but that is what real love does. How would you feel if God let everyone see your faults?

In *Peaceful Warrior,* Dan Millman says, "It seems that you take a lot for the sake of love, but sometimes the ones who are hardest to love are usually the ones who need it the most."

With that being said, even God has a limit. "Shall we continue in sin that grace may abound? Certainly not" (Romans 6:1).

God knows your heart. He knows when you are sincerely trying and when you are running game. It is not your call. He decides when your assignment is over.

In closing this section, I want to share a testimony that tells my experience with the love of God. The love draws, covers a multitude of sins (1 Peter 4:8), and casts out all fear (1 John 4:18).

> I accepted Christ when I was around eight years old. I remember going to church with Aunt Charity Little, Aunt Patricia Thomas, and then my mom. My life was filled with Sunday school, church service, evening service, Bible study, vacation Bible school, choir rehearsal, and the list goes on and on. However, when I left home to go to college, I stepped out of my walk with God and into my own little hell. I chose to stay there for a long time. Although I came back to Christ, I didn't really trust Him to be Lord in my life.

I still made decisions for myself without His guidance. To everyone looking in, I seemed "fine," but no one saw the tears I cried on my pillow.

One day, I woke up and realized I did not want the status quo. I didn't want to just exist. I wanted better and *greater* than before. Nothing was wrong, but I was irritated with where I was. It was a Pentecost Sunday. I sat in the service, but I didn't feel anything. I was just there.

I went home and contemplated not going back for the second service. I went anyway. I found my seat in a row and area I didn't usually sit in. As the praise team began to sing, I closed my eyes. The people and the room seemed to disappear. There was no one in the room except for God and me. It was as if I was in a room with the radio or TV on. I sat there for the whole service with God's arms wrapped around me. I put my head on His chest. There were no words spoken, but for the first time, I was open and vulnerable with my Savior. No mask, no agenda—just me. I didn't have to be a wife, mother, minister, or friend. I was just a daughter of the King. Where there was chaos and anxiety, peace now reigned.

Where there was doubt and fear, confidence and love resided. The same compassion I had given others was being showered upon me. God had invaded the room just for me. I'm sure He touched many people that night, but it was personal for me. I will never forget that defining moment. The night, I felt how much God loved me.

There was no burning bush, fireworks, thundering voices, or prophetic words. It was the humble quietness that I associate with Jesus. The love I felt was just a fact. However, the impact has changed my life dramatically. I was given an unbelievable thirst for really *knowing* my God and deeply desiring to live my life for His glory. This has certainly manifested itself in a change that can be seen, but I think *regeneration* is all about the change deep within me. There is no doubt that God has poured spiritual life into the "dead me" and given me a new life.

As much as I long for His glory and presence, there are still situations and days when I don't do so well. The difference is that I'm uncomfortable during those times. I don't like being there anymore. After that service, I had a newfound respect for the lyrics to

William McDowell's "Place of Worship." It was no longer about my husband, children, family, friends, or church. Everything was so clear, and it was all about God and me. Nothing else mattered. I had fallen in love with Him all over again. Tyler Perry wrote, "Love is stronger than any addiction. It is one." Instead of seeking the approval and love of people, I now crave the love of the Father.

♥ MY TRUTH

Let me start by saying that nothing I am sharing is to condemn my parents or to portray them in a bad light. They are great. I have a good relationship with them because of God's love and forgiveness, but I am sharing my stories to show how the enemy can use one incident to hold you hostage without you even realizing it.

I was born into a large family to a fourteen-year-old mother. My mom was always there, but I felt closer to my grandmother while I was growing up. My mom married a wonderful man who loved me and treated me as his own, but I spent most of my life desiring the love of my natural father. I felt rejected, unloved, and cast aside like no one wanted me. I had people around me who loved me, but I couldn't see or receive it because of one person missing from my life. I couldn't fathom the unconditional love of God or that a man could love me.

A seed was planted early on by the enemy, and I didn't love myself. I had taken all the hurt, shame, and disappointment of my parents (because they were so young) and placed it on my shoulders. I made it my own and I carried it for thirty-five years. Why? I internalized it. It became my drive to be an overachiever. I always felt that I had something to prove because I never felt validated. Honor student in high school, salutatorian in college, business owner, good job, and happy marriage—whatever I tried to do, I prospered, but I was empty inside and always longing. I was outwardly successful but inwardly miserable. I remember sitting in church and listening to them talk about the love of God. I thought, *He loves everyone but me. He'll do that for them, but I am exempt.* I didn't think I was meant to experience true happiness.

Let me jump ahead a moment. I was thirty-eight before I could look in the mirror and love the person looking back at me. I was deeply insecure. I had come to own it and wear it. It was part of my wardrobe. I just learned to cover it up well. It was like the layered effect when people get dressed.

I played the blame game for years, but in the end, I had to take responsibility for not seeking out the truth sooner for myself. Suffering in silence was/is not the best choice.

♥ YOUR TRUTH: *What does love mean to you in your life?*

_____

_____

_____

_____

_____

_____

_____

_____

_____

♥ GOD'S TRUTH

"Before I formed you in the womb I knew you, before you were born I set you apart" (Jeremiah 1:5 NIV).

"You saw me before I was born. Every day of my life was recorded in your book. Every moment was laid out before a single day had passed" (Psalm 139:16 NLT).

"For God so loved the world that He gave His only begotten Son, that whoever believes in Him should not perish but have everlasting life" (John 3:16 KJV).

♥ PRAYER

Lord, help me to understand and receive Your love—not what I have been taught by the world but Your agape love that never ends and never changes. The love that when I was still a sinner You allowed Your Son to die on the cross, sent the Holy Spirit to lead and guide me, and provided me with new grace and mercy every day. In a world full of chaos and letdowns, Your love never fails. I am thankful. Help me to understand the power love has to change the lives of others. In Jesus's name. Amen.

Chamber 2
FORGIVENESS

I was going through a rough patch emotionally. In two weeks, my family had buried two cousins. Some other things happened that did not sit well with me. I was beginning to let offense take root, but I turned to the Bible and sermons on the Internet for comfort.

One of the ministers was speaking, and he mentioned the art of forgiveness. As those four words kept ringing in my ear, it was as if a light bulb came on. Do you know the feeling when something moves from knowledge on paper or in a conversation to an actual revelation in your life? At that moment, I realized that forgiveness was a conscious choice. It wasn't something that just comes over you. It is something you have to work at and perfect.

When you wake up, choose not to replay what happened. Choose not to allow your emotions to control you. Choose to live a life that is pleasing to God. Is it an easy process? No. Anger and frustration are common emotions, but if they are not properly dealt with in the beginning, they can grow into rage.

Rage is like a cancer that eats away at everything it touches. One of the most profound statements to support the importance of forgiveness is found in Tyler Perry's *Diary of a Mad Black Woman*:

> I learned a long time ago that God can take care of folks far better than you can. If you got the opportunity to get even with someone that did you wrong and you don't take it, you are over it. If you beat the hell out of him you're not over it.
>
> You know I know this man put a hurtin' on you baby, but you've got to forgive him. No matter what he done, you've got to forgive him—not for him, but for you. Forgive him for me? When somebody hurts you, they take power over you. If you don't forgive them, then they keeps the power. Forgive him, baby, and after you forgive him, forgive yourself.[1]

---

1   *Diary of a Mad Black Woman*, dir. Darren Grant, writ. Tyler Perry, DVD, Tyler Perry Studios-Lionsgate Entertainment, 2005.

We've always heard about forgiving others, but why do you think we have to forgive ourselves? If we do not forgive ourselves and let go of what happened, we will paralyze ourselves. Have you ever seen the sci-fi movie where the people have flash frozen themselves so they could be thawed out later for some miracle cure or great event? "Unforgiveness" does the same thing. It stunts your growth emotionally and spiritually. You never grow past the time of offense. Have you ever seen a fifty-year-old react like an eight-year-old? Even with all our successes, our defense mechanisms, and walls we are still just a seven-, eight-, nine-, twelve-, or fifteen-year-old seeking love or approval. Acknowledge the pain—and forgive yourself today. There is nothing you could have done differently or better. God already knew what would happen before it happened, and He still loves you. It is up to you whether or not you allow situations in your life to be stumbling blocks or stepping-stones. Don't believe me? Take a look at Psalm 139:13–16 NLT.

> You made all the delicate, inner parts of my
> body and knit me together in my mother's
> womb.
> Thank you for making me so wonderfully
> complex!
> Your workmanship is marvelous—how well
> I know it.

You watched me as I was being formed in
utter seclusion, as I was woven together in
the dark of the womb.
You saw me before I was born.
Every day of my life was recorded in your
book.
Every moment was laid out before a single
day had passed.

This brings us to the final person you have to forgive.
After you forgive others and yourself, you have to forgive
God. Many would scoff at this statement, but have you
ever been mad at the death of a loved one or child? Have
you mourned the loss of innocence or a dream, looked
up to heaven, and said, "How could a loving God allow
this to happen?"

In life, you may feel that you have done nothing to
warrant what you are going through. How do you justify
the molestation of a child? The Bible says that God is
always there. Why didn't He stop it from happening?
God is a healer. How does a seven-year-old boy die from
cancer? Some situations hurt so badly that they cause you
to become angry and bitter enough to turn your back on
God. Imagine sitting in a doctor's office and hearing that
you may never be able to conceive a child. You may get
mad at the world, including God. Maybe you never said
it out loud, but you said it in your heart.

God knows the content and intent of our hearts, but He waits for us to be honest with Him about our feelings. I went through a situation that cost me a friendship, and then I had to swallow my pride. I had to give up my right for their wrong. I was right in everything I had done, but I had to grin and bear the ridicule. I could not retaliate. Did I know how? Yes. Did I have a few choice words I wanted to say? Yes. Was I mad with God? Yes. He was holding me to a higher standard. I had to extend something to these people that they did not extend to me—love, grace, and mercy—and I was mad about it! My pride was hurt. Things weren't going my way.

God had brought these people into my life, and here I was in this situation. After two weeks of my pity party, I broke. I was driving in my car and yelling, "I'm mad at you."

The gentlest voice said, "I know. Now we can talk."

Before that moment, I did not believe I could be honest with God about my anger, disappointments, frustrations, and all the negative things I felt. In that moment, I learned that God wanted to know everything about me. He could not help me forgive and get over that moment until I was honest about my feelings.

God began to show me the situation through His eyes, but I had to be in a position to see things differently. Pain and hurt will blind you. What once seemed like a deadly sword became divine protection. What was once a curse became a blessing to countless others when shared. Although He loves you, wants to dry all your tears, and wants to heal you, He cannot override your will. He waits patiently until you are ready to be honest, forgive, and receive His love—even when He didn't do anything wrong.

♥ MY TRUTH

This was the hardest chamber for me. I have a very good memory, and I was excellent at holding a grudge. I could remember what you did, where we were, what you said, and what you were wearing the day it happened. The sting stayed just as fresh. I got very good at not dealing with people. "Out of sight; out of mind" is not forgiveness. If I got mad at church, I left. If you hurt me, I cut you off. If I didn't like it, I just didn't deal with it.

The pain was still there, festering like an infection, and every time someone did or said something similar, all the feelings would come rushing back. I could go from zero to ninety like someone flipped a light switch. Hurt people hurt people. I avoided people because I didn't like conflict. I was very thankful for God's forgiveness, but growing up, I wasn't very free about sharing it with others. For many years I didn't turn the other cheek or restore my brother in love as the Bible commanded.

God convinced me by using my relationship with my husband. I couldn't cling to every wrong he ever did and then expect him to just forgive my mistakes. God said, "When you stop treating My people and Me like that, I will stop treating you that way." It was a hard pill to swallow. That was another one of my defense mechanisms to keep people from hurting me.

I learned to forgive my husband and look at every incident as the first time because we were both changing and evolving. I stopped using words like "you always" or "you never." I thought I was doing well, but then God sent me to a prophetic class. One of the lessons was on deliverance. As we sat there, the facilitator had us talk about our lives. I was willing to talk about everyone and everything but my father. When she hit that spot, I could feel my temperature change. I didn't want to be there anymore. I was putting a Band-Aid on an open wound, and she ripped it off.

The facilitator gave me an assignment to call my dad. I graciously declined. She insisted, and I agreed out of respect for God and her position. Everyone who knows me knows if I give my word, I will do it. However, that assignment was one of the hardest things I ever had to do. I didn't call him, but I did write a letter and placed it in the mail. My letter didn't condemn anyone, but I asked for a fresh start—and for him to have a relationship with my son.

After he received the letter, we talked. It was as if someone had lifted a weight off my shoulders. I was carrying something around that didn't belong to me. My perception was wrong, and the enemy had deceived me.

Not every situation will have a happy ending like mine. I have had to write several letters since that one. I never mailed them, but I had to get my feelings out. I had already forgiven God for my past when I forgave my father, but it took a while to forgive myself.

"Why didn't I say something sooner? I should have—"

We all say things to ourselves when we mess up. I didn't need anyone to put me down. I did it to myself (very well). Shortly after that incident, my father became sick and ended up in the hospital. How do you think I would have felt if I had not made things right? Thank You, God! I now have good relationships with my parents and my siblings because of forgiveness. I have also had to exhibit this when dealing with spiritual parents in ministry. Sometimes God released me, and sometimes I had to stay and be a big girl. I allowed God to grow me up, but the end was still the same. *Forgive them for how they hurt you, take responsibility for your part, and put your trust in God, where it belongs.*

In another instance, I remember talking to a coworker who was much older than me. She and her brother-in-law were not on speaking terms, and she felt justified in her behavior.

I said, "You can't get into heaven that way."

She looked at me and nodded.

I was sent to another site for a few weeks. Upon my return, I was met with the biggest hug and a card. I didn't understand this reaction. After further conversation, she revealed that she had talked to her brother-in-law and forgiven him after our conversation. Two weeks later, he passed away. All she could think about was how grateful she was that she did not have to carry that unforgiveness on her shoulders anymore. She was obedient to God, and she let it go.

♥ **YOUR TRUTH:** *How has unforgiveness affected your life?*

_____

_____

_____

_____

_____

_____

_____

_____

_____

♥ **GOD'S TRUTH**

"For if you forgive men when they sin against you, your Heavenly Father will also forgive you. But if you do not forgive men their sins, your Father will not forgive your sins" (Matthew 6:14–15 NIV).

"The Lord our God is merciful and forgiving, even though we have rebelled against him" (Daniel 9:9 NIV).

"And when you stand praying, if you hold anything against anyone, forgive him, so that your Father in heaven may forgive you your sins" (Mark 11:25 NIV).

"Repent, then, and turn to God, so that your sins may be wiped out, that times of refreshing may come from the Lord" (Acts 3:19 NIV).

♥ CALL TO ACTION

As an act of release, I want you to write a letter to the people you need to forgive (Mom, Dad, ex, Grandma, Grandpa, God, yourself) or buy a balloon that you can write on and release. On the balloon, write down all the hurt and emotions you feel. You don't have to give it to the person unless you are led to. Write it out, and release it to God.

❤ PRAYER

It's me, O Lord, standing in the need of prayer. I choose to forgive every person who has ever hurt me—from childhood until now. I allow You to pull back every hurt, layer by layer. As the layers come off, I am grateful for Your love, which acts as the healing balm of Gilead. I release them to be free so that I can live a full and happy life in Christ. In Jesus's name. Amen.

Chamber 3
TRUST

This chamber can be very difficult, but you must resist the urge to turn and run or hurry through the process. You must steady your course because this chamber has many levels. Have you ever seen a child being taught to walk or swim by a parent or a familiar adult? When the parent steps away, the child is afraid. Children believe (trust) that the parents will catch them if they fall. If the child sinks, the parent will go to the bottom of the pool to rescue the child.

We all start with the same childlike trust, but life happens. Someone hurt you, disappointed you, lied to you, or abused your trust. In those situations, you learn that trust is not freely given. It is earned. The Bible says, "Know them that labor among you and try the spirit by the spirit."

Trust is built in relationships. If you are not very good with natural relationships, I guarantee that you will have a hard time trusting God's love for you. How can a man you cannot see love you so much that He sent His only Son to die for you? All He asks in return is that you live for Him. Is this too good to be true? No, it is a fact. In the world, you can love without trust, but you cannot trust without love.

Do you have friends you love like family—or better than family—who you do not trust to take care of your children? How many of you will let them watch your children but will not tell them the intimate details of your heart? Some people close to you will never know your pain, disappointment, or heartache.

> "Guard your heart above all else, for it determines the course of your life" (Proverbs 4:23 NLT).

Many people have built their lives on this concept, and their hearts are hidden away from everyone—even God— like Fort Knox. We say that we love God, and I really believe that each of us does, but do we *trust* Him to be Lord and Savior in our lives? Do we trust Him to be?

- Jehovah Jireh Provider
- Jehovah Shalom Peace

- Jehovah Rapha Healer
- Jehovah Nissi Banner
- Jehovah Rohi Shepherd

If you never had a loving father, can you trust Him to be Abba Father in your life? Like the process of forgiveness, trust is a conscious choice. You have to choose to work at it. People will always be people, and as long as you are in this world, you will have tribulations. I wish I could tell you that no one will ever hurt you again.

I wish I could tell you that you will never be betrayed, talked about, or misunderstood. I cannot do that, but I can tell you that you do not have to dwell on those moments. You accept them for what they are—life lessons—and you keep moving. The moment you stop growing, changing, or maturing, you allow the other person or situation to take control of your life.

In this chamber, you learn to trust yourself *and* your relationship with God. Up until this point, you may have only known God as the children of Israel did: the God of Abraham, Isaac, and Jacob. In today's terms, the God of Great Grandma, Big Mama, and Mama. This is when God becomes real to you. This is the time when God starts transforming your mind. What do I mean?

When you really trust God—not just with your lips—He begins to show you the vision of what He has for your life. Well, you have to grow up to those visions. It starts out as something so overwhelming that it frightens you in most cases, but through experiences and situations, you grow into the vision. The vision doesn't change, but you do. You learn to trust God, yourself, and the God in others. This is the time when God will send other men and women of God to nurture and mentor you.

If you have a low trust factor, you will be suspect of their motives. There are people God ordained to help you reach your destination. They will be people of integrity and godly character who can be trusted and will love and support you right where you are. Trust is simply putting down your pride and allowing someone else to help you through this journey. Take inventory today and lighten the load. You are not an island; you are a member of the body of Christ created for a purpose.

❤ MY TRUTH

Because of life incidents, things I witnessed, and my insecurity, I did not trust people easily. I learned early on that when trust is broken you are not quick to give it again. There were always people around me, but there were not a lot of people in the inner parts of my heart. That was how I protected myself; I kept people at arm's length. If they wanted to leave, I wasn't attached. It took a lot for me to trust and open my heart, but when I did, it was for life.

When I did love and trust you, I loved wholeheartedly. There was nothing I wouldn't do for you, and the enemy knew that. I love to help people, but I want you to see the attacks of the enemy. He sent people on assignment who were very good at wading through all my defense mechanisms to get to my heart. Once they had infiltrated me, they used my heart against me. Do you know what happened? I shut down again, and it became a vicious cycle. I locked myself away from everyone, but no man is an island.

We all need others around us—whether we want to admit it or not. I had to learn that I didn't need everyone. I just needed God and those who could help me get to my destiny. I am not telling you to use people to get what you want. What I am saying is that God has ordained some people to be in your life to help you reach your maximum potential. It's a two-way street. You encourage one another, but you will miss the other person if you are not willing to open yourself up.

I am still cautious, and I do not wear my heart on my sleeve. God has recently brought two very special ladies into my life, and they are teaching me about "true godly friendship." We help each other, pray for each other, encourage each other, and respect our differences. They don't just withdraw; they are able to pour in. When there is a need, it is already there for them—and vice versa. We are so different but so alike, but do you know how I found them? I didn't. I allowed God to heal me and then I prayed. "God, send me the people who you want in my life."

Through trusting God to leave my job and volunteer, He brought these wonderful ladies into my life. We often marvel at how He orchestrated our steps. How do I trust this? A similar orchestration happened when I was young. I met my best friend, and we are still friends today.

I don't need a lot of friends. I just need the right ones, and like for all married people, my best friend is my mate. These relationships have been tested, but I am glad to say that some have stood the test of time. I still trust God and these people with my life.

♥ **YOUR TRUTH:** *Are you trusting of others and God?*

_____

_____

_____

_____

_____

_____

_____

_____

_____

_____

♥ **GOD'S TRUTH**

"Jesus Christ is the same yesterday and today and forever" (Hebrews 13:8 NIV).

"Do not throw away this confident trust in the Lord, no matter what happens. Remember the great reward it brings you! You need to persevere so that when you have done the will of God, you will receive what he has promised" (Hebrews 10:35–36 NLT).

"This truth gives them confidence that they have eternal life, which God—who does not lie—promised them before the world began" (Titus 1:2 NLT).

❤ PRAYER

Help me to trust in the Lord with all my heart and not lean to my own understanding. Don't allow me to go to what is familiar. Help me be open to the people who You are bringing into my life. You know what and who I need in order to reach my destination. With You as my guide, I cannot go wrong. Teach me balance. Even though these awesome people are coming into my life, You are front and center in my life. You are the reason I have my being, Lord. You are my first love, my friend. Once I trust You, I can truly learn to trust others. And for those who have been removed from my life, help me to continue to walk in forgiveness and love—even when it hurts. In Jesus's name. Amen.

Chamber 4
ABUNDANT LIFE

It is not the strongest of the species that survive, nor the most intelligent, but the one most responsive to change.
—Charles Darwin

You have learned to love God's way. You have forgiven others, yourself, and God. You have left your pride at the door, and you trust God to navigate your life and bring the right people your way to help you. Your mind has been transformed. Your thoughts line up with His thoughts. Now you exit into abundant life.

When you hear the word *abundance,* your mind automatically thinks of money. That is a part of it, but that is not where it begins or ends. True abundance is walking in the will and favor of God. You go to a place where people don't see you without seeing the hand of

God on your life. Abundance is spiritual and physical health.

> "Brethren, I wish above all that you would prosper and be in good health even as your soul prospers" (1 John 3).

Don't believe me? Ask a person who has cancer what they would give to have their health. In 2013, we buried our godson at the age of eight. He lost the battle to cancer, but he won the war with God. We knew how Adonte had touched our lives, but at his funeral, we saw his impact on others. God had used his life to bring us all together from all walks of life and races. He didn't have any riches or money, but he was the richest person in that room in love.

I encourage you today to look around and take inventory in your own life. Look at what is truly important. Laugh a little louder. Love a little harder. Don't forget to live with purpose. Don't wait to do something on your bucket list. That is what I learned from Adonte: tomorrow is not promised.

❤ MY TRUTH

I was sitting with a friend at lunch, and I was explaining how God was blessing my family. I was not working anymore, but the house was taken care of—and we were happier than we had ever been.

She looked at me and said, "You do realize you are living an abundant life."

I sat there and began to ponder that statement. I reflected on how long we had struggled to get something—and we had everything we needed. We knew what true happiness felt like. We don't put off for tomorrow what we could do today. We dealt with problems and situations immediately instead of letting them fester and grow.

We are learning to enjoy the moment instead of spending a lifetime hoping. We don't settle anymore, and we hold fast to the promises of God over our lives. Not everything is *perfect,* but it is *really* good. Do we have bad days? Yes, but we keep moving forward and trusting God.

❤ **YOUR TRUTH:** *Is abundant life within your reach?*

_____

_____

_____

_____

_____

_____

_____

_____

_____

_____

❤ **GOD'S TRUTH**

> "You will make known to me the path of life; in your presence is fullness of joy; in your right hand there are pleasures forever" (Psalm 16:11 ESV).

"Sing to the Lord; praise the Lord! For he has delivered the life of the needy from the hand of evildoers" (Jeremiah 20:13 ESV).

"And you will know the truth, and the truth will set you free" (John 8:32 ESV).

♥ PRAYER

Lord, help me see what You see and desire what You desire for my life. You have ordained for us to be whole and full until we overflow. Psalm 23 states, "My cup runs over." My cup runs over with joy, peace, love, meekness, gentleness, and the other fruits of the Holy Spirit. My body overflows with healing, and every limb functions in the perfection in which You created it to function. My bank account overflows so that I may be a blessing to the kingdom of God. My job overflows because the favor of the Lord follows me wherever I go. Everything in my life will line up with what the Word of God says because I decree and declare it to be so. In Jesus's name. Amen.

SHAKEN

What should you do when the foundation is shaken and the floor falls out from under you? Remember that this is a journey. You can do all the right things, and bad things can still happen. You followed all the steps and trusted God with your whole heart (or as much as you could give at the time) and bam!

What do I mean? Everyone will face situations in life that shake the foundation of who they are and their walk with God. It can be a divorce, a relationship that doesn't end well, the loss of a loved one, leaving a church you love, or an illness. The situation will be different for each and every one of you, but the feelings will be the same. You can't breathe. You can't read your Bible. You can't pray. You are numb. You feel like God has deserted you, and everything that you have done or believed was a lie.

I come to bring you hope in this hour. God has not deserted you, and He meant every word He ever spoke to you and about you. As I sit here, I am reminded of a story that I read years ago. "The Eagle's Molt" explains how this beautiful majestic bird goes through a season where it cannot fly or see, and it is completely dependent upon others for its livelihood. During this process, the eagle is vulnerable and retreats to a safe place. This is what we do too. It feels like you are starting over, but let me just give you a nugget now. Once the process is over, his vision is sharper and his wings are stronger than before. I cannot keep you from going through the process, but maybe I can help you endure. The key is to not stop, give up, or quit.

You must get up every day. I am not talking about getting up and murmuring or complaining. You must get up, brush your teeth, take a bath, get dressed, talk to God, and listen to worship music or sermons. There was a season when I couldn't read the Word of God, but I listened to the online Bible, sermon tapes, and worship music. It nourished and cleansed my soul until I had the strength to feed myself (2 Chronicles 20:20).

Speak life, and if you cannot speak life, keep your mouth shut. Your negative words will prolong the process (Deuteronomy 30:19; Proverbs 18:21).

Accept responsibility for your actions. This is not a time to focus on what someone else did to you. This is the time to see what has attracted the person to you. *What part did I play in this situation? Did I consult God? Did I trust God—or was I looking for man to do only what God can do?* This season forces you to look deep inside yourself. If you cannot see your part in the situation, you can never move forward. No matter what a person does to you, you are ultimately responsible for your actions because you have a choice whether to stay or go (Galatians 6:7–10).

Don't be afraid of the process of change. Change is a word we don't like very much because we live our lives while trying to be comfortable. We are afraid to push the envelope and step outside our comfort zones. Sometimes God allows things to happen to force us to move. God doesn't deal in comfort with our walk with Christ. God wants us to be hot or cold—not lukewarm. Many of us are comfortable with God restoring us to our former states (salvation), but we have a problem with God promoting us to the next level. Promotion brings new responsibilities and duties that we often think we are not qualified to do. This is when we go back to the trust factor. We must realize that during this process of change, God is redefining who we are. He knows the treasure He has placed inside these earthen vessels, and He knows what it will take for it to be revealed. In this instance, we must trust the master craftsman and learn to celebrate ourselves. Do not be prideful, but be confident in who you are in God (Psalm 23:4).

Learn to build fences not walls. Take a moment to close your eyes and create a mental picture of a wall and a fence. Did you notice that most fences are made from wood or iron, but walls are made of cement? Fences are made to be moved or expanded, and walls are built to be permanent. A fence can be torn down or moved with normal, everyday tools, and walls require heavy-duty equipment.

Wikipedia states that a defensive wall functions as a fortification used to defend a city or settlement from potential aggressors. In ancient to modern times, they were used to enclose settlements. When the enemy would come, they would lock the gate so no one could go in or out of the city. The only people who could see outside were posted in the watchtower. If they decided an incoming visitor was friendly, they would sound the alarm for the gate to be opened. If the visitor was deemed hostile, they were kept on the outside. It kept enemies out, but it also kept the people of the city hostage. No one came in, but they could not go out either.

You may or may not remember the story of the Berlin Wall. This infamous wall was constructed by the government in 1961 and separated East Berlin from West Berlin. Family units were separated and destroyed because of this wall. In 1989 after the erosion of political power in East Germany and weeks of civil unrest, the government allowed its residents to visit West Germany and West Berlin.

A fence, on the other hand, is not completely restrictive. It can be knocked down, jumped over, or moved with minimal effort. Some protection is necessary, but never let it isolate you. An idle mind is truly the devil's workshop. He is the father of lies, and he will feed your thoughts until you come into agreement with him.

> "Above all else, guard your heart for everything you do flows from it" (Proverbs 4:23 NIV).

"A heart at peace gives life to the body but envy rots the bones" (Proverbs 14:30 NIV).

"A happy heart makes the face cheerful, but heartache crushes the spirit" (Proverbs 15:13 NIV)

"A cheerful heart is good medicine, but a crushed spirit dries up the bones" (Proverbs 17:22 NIV).

❤ MY TRUTH:

In September 2010, I went to a women's conference in Destin, Florida. It was beautiful, and the ladies were so nice. On the first night, I was enjoying the worship experience and interacting with others from all over the world. I don't remember the minister's name, but I remember the message: *living life without walls.*

I realized I did not know how to do that. I had lived by "protecting myself" from others. I loved others and would move the world for them, but I did not let other people—including my husband—know the inner secrets of my heart. I did not go to the altar for prayer that night, but I went the following night. Do you know who was there to greet me? Yes, the minister from the night before.

I had to confess to her that I did not know how to live the life she had preached about the night before.

She prayed that God would teach me how and that I would learn to trust again. At the time of this writing (July 2013), it has been almost three years but I am happy to report that the walls have steadily come down. I share these dates to show that not everything is instantaneous. I did not build the walls overnight, and it would be unrealistic to think they would come down overnight.

As each brick came down, I had to develop a certain level of security. I had to feel safe. I recently went on vacation with my father's side of the family, and as we got ready to leave, I hugged him as I always did. However, I could feel his heart that time. I could feel the love and validation. I realized it had been there all along, but I had been so guarded that I couldn't receive it or see it. Why? I couldn't receive what I wasn't willing to give to myself first. My own defenses were holding me hostage. Now that they are gone, I am free to love myself—and others—without any secret expectations.

♥ **YOUR TRUTH:** *Is your life lived behind walls or a fence?*

_____

_____

_____

_____

_____

_____

_____

_____

_____

_____

♥ **GOD'S TRUTH**

"The name of the Lord is a fortified tower; the righteous run to it and are safe" (Proverbs 18:10 NIV).

"Now the gates of Jericho were tightly shut because the people were afraid of the Israelites. No one was allowed to go out or in" (Joshua 6:1 NLT).

"There is no fear in love. But perfect love drives out fear, because fear has to do with punishment. The one who fears is not made perfect in love" (1 John 4:18, NIV).

Receive God's help and those who He sends to minister to you. This does not refer to the normal people you would seek out but to those people who can help you walk through this process. Word of caution—do not make these people gods in your life. Always keep your focus on God.

Get into a great local church. This is not necessarily the place your mom and grandma attended, but this will be a place where you feel the presence of God. They will nurture you as a person—not just your gift. They will love you unconditionally and push you beyond your limits. They want what God wants for your life—with no benefit for themselves. Find a shepherd with the heart of God for His people instead of someone who speaks eloquently and sells get-rich-quick schemes. Make sure you are in a place that is conducive for your season. They should not allow you to be comfortable, but they should push you to be better. In this place, you can be a servant like Jesus Christ was while here on earth.

Don't forget what you already know: love, forgive, trust, and end in abundant life. This is a beautiful cycle that is like the interworking of the natural heart. The blood is carried through the veins into the different sections of the heart. In life, we continually have to draw from these four chambers of God's heart to survive. Remember you are just being shaken so that anything that is not connected can fall off instead of stirred where you force things that don't want to combine to come together. Nothing from this season that is not a part of your destiny can stay.

♥ MY TRUTH

I have had several times when the ground was shaken under me. In high school, my self-esteem was so low that I did not want to live anymore. Every day, I thought about how everyone would be better off without me and how nobody would miss me. In college, I was almost a victim of date rape. I was somewhere I had no business being with someone I thought I could trust. He and his friends tormented me for days. It got to the point where I wouldn't eat if they were in the cafeteria. I avoided all the places they would be because I was afraid.

Another time, I went to the doctor, and they said we would not be able to have children without fertility treatments. I also found out that my pastor had been propositioning members of the church and gossiping with them. I defended them, served them, and loved them, and they turned on me and crucified me. I had no agenda. I just had my love for God.

Maybe the hardest time was in 2013 when we buried my godson, my uncle, a family friend, and my grandmother between February 1 and March 16. I can see God's hands in each of these situations. He kept me even when I wasn't saved and couldn't keep myself. In the earlier situations, my recovery time wasn't as strong. I didn't have peace, and I would have a lot of pity parties.

I have learned to trust God, and He has given me a peace that surpasses all understanding. I have my moments, but I don't stay there. My recovery time for trusting God and standing on a firm foundation has improved. With every test, I learn more about who God is in my life. I depend more on my gentle guide, the Holy Spirit.

♥ **YOUR TRUTH:** *How has your world been shaken?*

_____

_____

_____

_____

_____

_____

_____

_____

_____

♥ GOD'S TRUTH:

"'For I know the plans I have for you,' declares the Lord, 'plans to prosper you and not to harm you, plans to give you hope and a future'" (Jeremiah 29:11 NIV).

"'For a brief moment I abandoned you, but with deep compassion, I will bring you back. In a surge of anger, I hid my face from you for a moment, but with everlasting kindness I will have compassion on you,' says the Lord your redeemer" (Isaiah 54:7–8 NIV).

"The Lord blessed the latter part of Job's life more than the first ... After this, Job lived a hundred and forty years; he saw his children and their children to the fourth generation. And so he died, old and full of years" (Job 42:12–16 NIV).

♥ PRAYER

Lord, help me remember that life will happen. Some things will be by choice, and others will be by design. No matter the cause, You will never leave me or forsake me. In the moments when You seem distant or silent, let me trust You even more. Consume me so that when the winds and the waves come to shake me, I will be able to stand on a firm foundation … the rock of ages, Jesus Christ. I do not have to build walls to protect myself anymore because You are my protector and the lifter of my head. You are my fence, my hedge of protection. When I am afraid, the Word of God says You are a strong tower; the righteous run in, and they are safe. I stand and declaring the words from Job. I say, "Though he slay me, yet will I trust him." Thank You for leading and guiding me through every storm that may arise in my life and providing every provision needed. In Jesus's name. Amen.

On April 28, 2012, I stood up. Remember my original vision? Once you enter this process, you can't stand in the love chamber, the forgiveness chamber, or the trust chamber. You were only able to stand when you had passed into abundant life. That is where you are not looking at things from a distorted or fragmented view that is caused by hurt. In there, you love God with your whole heart—and not through your natural eyes and experiences. You are healed.

This journey has been long, and I am not where I want to be. I am right where I am *supposed* to be. As I was driving down the interstate to prayer, I asked God why I did not have the same feelings about church as I normally do. I asked, "Why don't I have my pastor's heart?"

He said, "Because you have mine. You finally understand what it means to have the heart of God. Now you can proceed to abundant life."

My heart skipped a beat, and I knew my passage through the chambers was finally over. I would not change anything for the wisdom, knowledge, and maturity that have been gained through this process. I continue to grow in my love for God every day because we never stop using the lessons we have learned. I thought this would be the end, but there was much more to learn. This entrance into abundant life brought my final lesson: don't settle.

Growing up in church, I was very familiar with the scripture that says, "Be ye transformed by the renewing of your mind." I entered into this new place with God, but I had been in that old position for so long that I was afraid to move forward. I was afraid to enjoy life and give of myself again.

I had gotten so comfortable in my process that I almost missed the destination. I was so used to not enough and just enough that more than enough seemed out of reach. Things were good, but God wanted my life to be great! I didn't have to accept what people said I could have. I could possess what the King said I could have. To settle means to adopt a steadier or more secure style of life, especially in a permanent job or home. This is the difference between a retirement account funded by stocks or bonds. I remember looking at my retirement account and my husband's account. I had worked and contributed to my retirement account for thirteen years, but he had tripled my investment. Why? My contributions were in a balanced fund with a few stocks and bonds to balance it out. It was conservative. My husband's account was all stocks. He was seeing the benefits of being aggressive.

When you settle and take a conservative approach, you may not lose anything—but you won't gain a lot either. Sometimes you have to put it all in. You have to have the faith of Abraham when God told him to leave his father's house and country and go to a place God would show him. What about having Isaac give the wells to the Philistines and building more and being more prosperous. God is not trying to take what we have; He is trying to get so much more to us. He doesn't just want to be Jehovah Jireh. He wants to be the God of more than enough. God can do exceedingly and abundantly above all that we ask or think. On July 7, 2013, I began to walk in my God-given authority and victory.

❤ MY TRUTH

My early years were spent not wanting to be a statistic. Many family members said I would be pregnant by the age of sixteen because I was born to a teenage mother. I achieved that goal, and then I wanted to live the life that my parents had—the house, the cars, and the kids. I was scared to push the envelope because I didn't want to fail or disappoint anyone. I existed in my own little world, watching my life pass me by.

One day, I realized that my parents weren't the destination. They were a springboard for me. I should accomplish more than they did, and my children should accomplish more than me. Until my mind-set changed, I couldn't receive God's abundant life or His plans for me. I would always settle for what was convenient or comfortable, which normally kept me or led me outside of the will of God. Most of the things God has ordained for my life have required me to live outside my comfort zone.

♥ **YOUR TRUTH:** *How are you settling in your life?*

_____

_____

_____

_____

_____

_____

_____

_____

_____

_____

♥ **GOD'S TRUTH:**

"Do not remember the past events, pay no attention to things of old. Look, I am about to do something new" (Isaiah 43:18–19 Holman Christian Standard Bible).

"Let us throw off everything that hinders and the sin that so easily entangles, and let us run with perseverance the race marked out for us" (Hebrews 12:1 NIV).

"I have been reminded of your sincere faith, which first lived in your grandmother Lois and in your mother Eunice, and I am persuaded, now lives in you also. For this reason, I remind you to fan into flame [stir up] the gift of God, which is in you" (2 Timothy 1:5–6 NIV).

"Now to him who is able to do immeasurably more than all we ask or imagine, according to his power that is at work within us, to him be glory in the church and in Christ Jesus throughout all generations, forever and ever!" (Ephesians 3:20 NIV).

❤ PRAYER

Lord, help me see what You see and desire what You desire for my life. Let me not stop moving from glory to glory. Help me always remember that You are faithful and just to complete the work that You have begun in me to give me an expected end. You are the one who makes us rich and adds no sorrow. As long as I keep my eyes and my faith on You, I can't fail. The only way that I don't win is if I stop. Stopping is not an option. From this day forth, I will press on with the tenacity of a bulldog. I will hold on to every word that God has spoken over my life. I will not settle for second best or less than exceedingly abundantly above what I can ask or even think of because I am a child of God. A new boldness comes upon me today to run on now that I understand the heart of God and know of His undying love for me. In Jesus's name. Amen.

CONCLUSION

*A*s long as we have breath, life will continue to happen—and we will have new revelations of God and ourselves. During these times, you have to remember to love, forgive, and trust. Do not retreat. We should always strive to be better than we were the day before, and that is only accomplished through constant evaluation.

In our society, if you get a cold or headache, you take a pill. Is that pill masking the symptoms of a deeper problem or curing the problem? In life, we no longer want to put a Band-Aid on a bullet wound to mask the symptoms; we are going to get to the root of the matter by understanding God's love for us. When we truly understand His love, we will accept that we don't have to be perfect or supercompetitive.

All that is required is that you are the best you that you can be. Stop limiting yourself, and move forward in the life God has set out before you. Don't be afraid to ask for help along the way (counseling or just a friendly chat). There will be bumps, bruises, and detours, but you are equipped for the journey.

On the next page, I encourage you to write out a bucket list (by faith) of things you want to see on this next leg of your journey. I am not asking you to write what you are qualified to do or can afford to do. Write down the desires of your heart, and believe in God for abundant life.

BUCKET LIST

_____

_____

_____

_____

_____

_____

_____

_____

_____

_____

_____

_____

_____

_____

_____

_____

_____

_____

_____

_____

*That moment when you realize your heart is open and
the only limits you have are the ones in your own mind.*
—Cassandra Williams

RESOURCES

Here is a list of books, music, phone apps, and movies that have helped me—and continue to help me—along this journey. God can use many different avenues to help bring about the healing that is needed in the lives of His people. He will meet you wherever you are—even in a movie theater.

❤ BOOKS

- *'Til the Last Drop,* Pastor Marquis Boone
- *The Bait of Satan,* John Bevere
- *The Assignment,* Mike Murdock
- *Digging Up Roots,* A. Nicole Alexander
- *Instinct,* Bishop T. D. Jakes

♥ MUSIC

- Myles and DeLana, Rutherford Driven
- William Murphy III
- Williams McDowell
- Tamela Mann
- Hill Song
- Casting Crowns
- Smokie Norful

♥ PHONE APPS

- YouVersion (Bible App)

♥ MOVIES

- *Blessed and Cursed*, 2010, Joel Kapity
- *Peaceful Warrior,* 2006, Victor Salva
- *The Karate Kid,* 2010, Harald Zwart
- *The Book of Eli,* 2010, The Hughes Brothers
- *The Lego Movie,* 2014, Phil Lord and Christopher Miller
- *Horton Hears a Who,* 2008, Jimmy Hayward and Steve Martino
- *Premonition*, 2007, Mennan Yapo

- *Faith Like Potatoes,* 2006, Regardt van den Bergh
- *Facing Giants,* 2006, Alex Kendrick
- *X-Men*, 2000, Brian Singer
- *Transformers,* 2007, Michael Bay